ALL ABOUT...

THE COMING OF THE

RAILWAYS

PAM ROBSON

Text © Pam Robson 1996

Illustrations © Dez Marwood 1996

Photographs © Sources credited

© Macdonald Young Books Ltd 1996

First published in Great Britain in 1996 by Macdonald Young Books

61 Western Road, Hove, East Sussex, BN3 1JD

A CIP catalogue for this book is available from the British Library.

ISBN 0 7500 1826 7 (hbk) 0 7500 1937 9 (pbk)

Editor: Annie Scothern

Designer: Jane Hannath

Picture credits: Science and Society Picture Library - *cover, title page, 7, 9b, 10, 11, 12, 14, 15, 16, 17, 18, 20, 22, 24, 25, 26, 27, 28bl, 29, 31, 34, 36br, 37, 39*. Mary Evans Picture Library - *8, 9t, 13, 28br, 32, 36bl, 42, 43*. Beamish Museum - *19b*. Durham County Council, Arts, Libraries and Museums Department - *21*. Thomas Cook Travel Archive - *30*. Mainstream Photography - *35*. Milepost 92½ - *38*. ET Archive - *40*. The Queensland Tourist and Travel Corporation - *41*. National Gallery - *45t*. Bluebell Railway - *45b*.

The author and publishers thank the above for permission to reproduce their photographs.

Printed and bound in Belgium by Proost N.V.

Other titles in the *ALL ABOUT...* series:

THE GREAT PLAGUE

THE GREAT FIRE OF LONDON

THE FIRST WORLD WAR

ALL ABOUT...

THE COMING OF THE
RAILWAYS

PAM ROBSON

The Pleasures of the Rail-Road. — Showing the Inconvenience of a Blow up.

MACDONALD YOUNG BOOKS

TIMELINE

1694 *London's first taxi service – horse-drawn hackney carriages*

1698 *Thomas Savery's steam pumping machine*

1712 *Thomas Newcomen's steam engine*

1758 *The first Railway Act in Britain*

1761 *The first canal in Britain – the Bridgewater Canal*

1788 *James Watt's steam engine*

1802 *Albert Mathieu's proposal for the first Channel Tunnel*

1808 *Richard Trevithick's* Catch-me-who-can *portable steam engine*

1813 Puffing Billy – *the oldest surviving steam railway locomotive*

1825 Locomotion No.1 *runs on the Stockton to Darlington public railway*

1827 *Timothy Hackworth builds the* Royal George

1829 *Rainhill trials won by Stephenson's* Rocket

1830 *The first steam passenger railway service – Liverpool to Manchester*

1836 *Canada's first steam railway*

1841 *Thomas Cook's first British travel agency*

1844 *Railways Act – rail companies in Britain had to run one train a day on each of their lines at a cost of a penny a mile*

1851 *The Great Exhibition opens in London*

1863 *The first underground rail system – London's Metropolitan Railway*

1869 *Completion of the first railway line across USA*

1873 *Opening of the Midland Grand Hotel at St. Pancras Station in London*

1890 *First electric 'tube' train in London*

1898 *Diesel engine patented by Dr Rudolph Diesel*

1938 Mallard *reaches a speed of 126 mph*

1948 *Nationalisation of the railways in Britain*

1984 *Closure of the world's first railway wagon works in north-east England*

1994 *Opening of the Channel Tunnel*

CONTENTS

THERE'S NO FUTURE FOR THE RAILWAYS — THE HUMAN BODY WOULD DISINTEGRATE AT SPEEDS ABOVE 30 M.P.H!

THE TRAIN NOW ARRIVING...

Today we take for granted our rigidly timetabled public transport services – buses, trains and tubes. When a train arrives late, passengers express their annoyance, sometimes quite loudly. Imagine a time when timetables were impossible – not only was transport too slow but each part of Britain also had its own local time! This was the situation before the railways arrived.

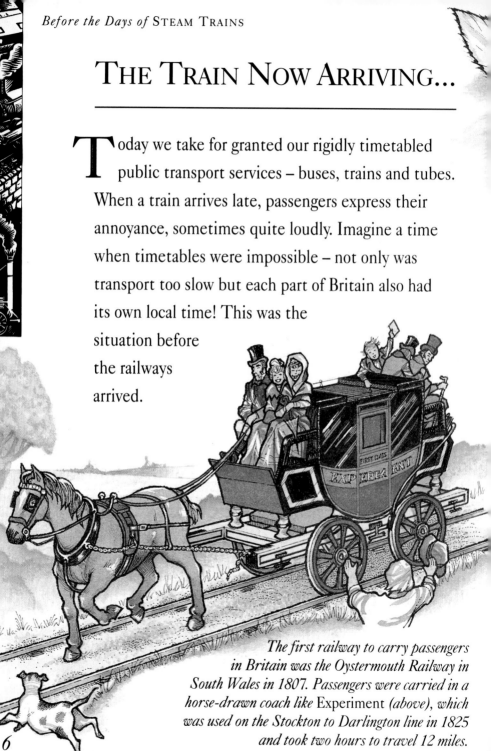

The first railway to carry passengers in Britain was the Oystermouth Railway in South Wales in 1807. Passengers were carried in a horse-drawn coach like Experiment *(above), which was used on the Stockton to Darlington line in 1825 and took two hours to travel 12 miles.*

In 1802 Albert Mathieu proposed a tunnel under the English Channel through which horse-drawn carriages would travel.

Nowadays we can travel anywhere in the world by plane, boat or train. Even space travel is possible. Britain's isolation from the Continent has vanished with the opening of the Channel Tunnel. Passengers can now travel by train from London to Paris in just three hours.

The Channel Tunnel's high-speed trains link Britain to the Continental rail network. Most capital cities on the European mainland can now be reached from London within a day.

INNS ALONG THE WAY

London's taxi service began in 1694 with an Act of Parliament that permitted 250 horse-drawn hackney carriages

A horse-drawn omnibus (1836).

to ply for trade. By 1825 a public passenger railway service was operating in the coalfields of north-east England, but the 'railway coach' was still pulled by horses. At that time horses were still the only reliable source of power for local and long-distance journeys. The years between 1800 and 1830 were the 'golden age' of stagecoaches in Britain. Around 1,000 left

London daily to travel the newly improved roads.

Inns offered resting 'stages' for coaches every seven miles along the route. Fresh horses were provided – four or six were needed for each stagecoach.

Each parish had to pay for the upkeep of its roads, so toll-gates were set up on the busiest routes. Travellers had to pay to pass.

The journey from London to Birmingham now took only half a day. Mail coaches were able to travel day and night at great speeds of 19 mph. In 1829 the first horse-drawn omnibuses were seen.

Strange steam-powered carriages appeared in the streets (1827). People were afraid of them so they soon went out of use.

CANALS AT WORK

From 1750 onwards, dramatic changes took place in Britain. Industry expanded and the Factory Age began. Great technological advances were made and there was a population explosion. Manufacturing towns near to the iron industries and coalfields grew rapidly. Rural workers, forced from the newly enclosed farms, went to the towns to work in factories and mines.

A rural scene is threatened by smoking furnaces. This painting of 1801 shows the changes brought by the Industrial Revolution.

The canals were dug by navvies (labourers), who bored tunnels and built aqueducts to create a network of canals throughout Britain.

Opened in 1761, the Bridgewater Canal between Worsley and Manchester was the first canal to be built in Britain.

The Industrial Revolution, as it is now known, changed people's lives and methods of work forever. Before the railways arrived, goods like coal and iron had to be hauled along canals by horse-drawn barges. In 1825 there were 1,000 miles of navigable waterways in Britain and heavy goods could be carried fairly quickly and cheaply. But the railways were soon to take this haulage trade from the barges.

THE POWER OF STEAM

Before the Industrial Revolution in Britain, only natural sources of power had been available – wind and water. But windmills and waterwheels can only be sited in certain places. Steam power made industry possible because steam engines can be used anywhere, if there is a constant supply of coal. Steam power was not new in the 1800s – steam engines had first been developed to pump water from coalmines over 100 years before. The two main factors that brought about the revolution in industry were coal and iron.

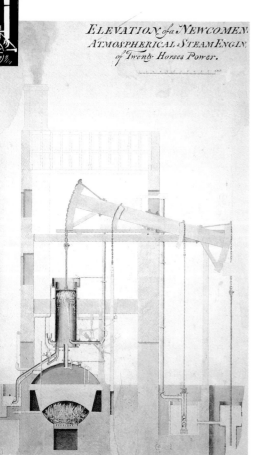

ELEVATION of a NEWCOMEN ATMOSPHERICAL STEAM ENGIN of Twenty Horses Power.

Thomas Newcomen (1663-1729) invented a machine that worked a pump instead of lifting the water as Savery's had done. This was the first successful steam engine. Built in 1712, it was first used in tin mines in the west of England.

Children were employed to pull trucks in coalmines.

As the demand for coal increased, mines had to be dug deeper and pumping water out of them became a serious problem. In 1698 Thomas Savery patented his steam pumping machine. He described its task as: "...the Raiseing of Water...by the impellant Force of Fire."

The new steam engines worked more powerfully and steadily than the old-style waterwheels.

13

HAULING COAL

I n 1808 Richard Trevithick developed a portable steam engine. People paid one shilling (12d) to see *Catch-me-who-can* go round a circular enclosure in London. But the real start of the railway revolution in Britain took place in north-east England, at Wylam Colliery.

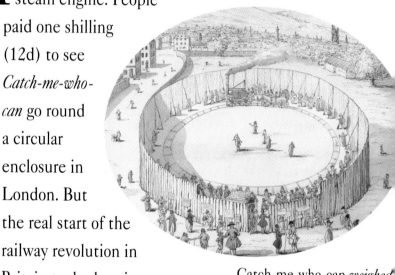

Catch-me-who-can *weighed eight tons and reached a speed of 12 mph.*

Puffing Billy *hauled coal wagons at a walking pace (just like this engine) between Wylam Colliery and the river Tyne for 48 years.*

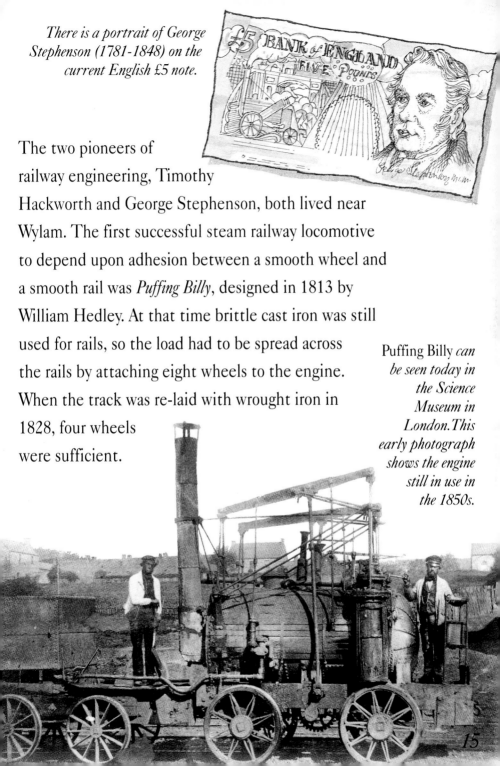

The two pioneers of railway engineering, Timothy Hackworth and George Stephenson, both lived near Wylam. The first successful steam railway locomotive to depend upon adhesion between a smooth wheel and a smooth rail was *Puffing Billy*, designed in 1813 by William Hedley. At that time brittle cast iron was still used for rails, so the load had to be spread across the rails by attaching eight wheels to the engine. When the track was re-laid with wrought iron in 1828, four wheels were sufficient.

Puffing Billy can be seen today in the Science Museum in London. This early photograph shows the engine still in use in the 1850s.

TRACKS TO MOVE ALONG

The wheel was invented by the Sumerians in the 4th century BC. Its first use was probably as a potter's wheel, in a horizontal position. The vertical use of the wheel brought about a major change in the movement of people and goods. The first wheels were made from wood but the metal wheel was soon developed. Then rails were laid for wheeled vehicles to move along. Rail tracks and

This 16th-century picture is evidence of an early European rail track.

wheeled vehicles may have been used as early as the 12th century in German mines. These 'permanent ways' were in use, underground, in the mines of north-east England in the 16th century. Sledges or wheelbarrows were moved along wooden rails. By the 17th century rail tracks were also in use above ground. Soon cast-iron tracks were laid but were replaced with wrought iron and then with steel by 1880.

The first Railway Act in Britain (1758) for the construction of a railway between Leeds and Middleton, in northern England.

An ACT for Establishing Agreements made between Charles Brandling, Esquire, and other Persons, Proprietors of Lands, for laying down a Waggon-Way, in order for the better supplying the Town and Neighbourhood of Leeds, in the County of York, with Coals.

Whereas Charles Brandling, Esquire, Lord of the Manor of Middleton, in the County of York, is Owner and Proprietor of divers Coal-works, Mines, Veins, and Seams of Coals, lying and being within the said Manor of Middleton, and Places adjacent ; and hath proposed, and is willing to engage and undertake, to furnish and supply the Inhabitants of the Town of Leeds with Coals for their necessary Use and Consumption, at the Rate or Price of Four Pence Three Farthings a Corf, containing in Weight about Two hundred and Ten Pounds, and in Measure Seven thousand Six

These quarry trucks from the 1730s moved along rails to carry stones to the river. Gravity pulled the loaded truck down, while a man walking behind controlled the brake. A horse then pulled the empty truck back up the hill.

17

A Daily Passenger Service

O n 27 September 1825 George Stephenson drove his *Locomotion No. 1* steam engine for 12 miles, pulling a carriage of passengers and 12 wagons laden with coal and flour. Royal assent had been given for the Stockton and Darlington Railway to be built in northern England and the rails had been laid in 1822. The original purpose of the line had been to carry coal in horse-drawn wagons from the mines near Shildon, via Darlington, for shipment on the river Tees at Stockton. A new assent had to be obtained to allow the use of locomotives on the line. *Locomotion No. 1*'s first run was a great success, but it was not until 1834 that locomotives replaced horses as a cheaper form of transport for both passengers and goods.

An early timetable for the short local journey.

Locomotion No.1 *passing a stagecoach on the day the railway opened.*

The first regular passenger service between Stockton and Darlington in October 1825 was the daily horse-drawn railway coach called *Experiment*.

This working replica of Locomotion No.1 *with a chauldron wagon was built for the 150th anniversary of the Stockton and Darlington Railway. The original engine is in the Darlington Railway Museum.*

'THE FATHER OF THE LOCOMOTIVE'

Timothy Hackworth (1786-1850)

Historians disagree about who should be called 'The father of the locomotive'. Most people believe it should be George Stephenson, but there are also many who would give the title to Timothy Hackworth – the engine superintendent on the Stockton and Darlington Railway. A staunch Methodist, he refused to work on Sundays and was responsible for the growth of Methodism in the area.

5
ROYAL GEORGE

In 1828 the Royal George *carried 22,442 tons over 20 miles at a cost of £466. The same amount of work using horse power would have cost £998. This amazing engine travelled at 9 mph.*

The Shildon railway works begun by Hackworth were the first of their kind in the world. They were closed in 1984.

In 1827 at the railway works in Shildon, Hackworth built the *Royal George* – the first locomotive capable of working more cheaply than horses. Hackworth then decided to enter the locomotive competition organised by the Liverpool and Manchester Railway in 1829, but his engine *Sans Pareil* was unsuccessful.

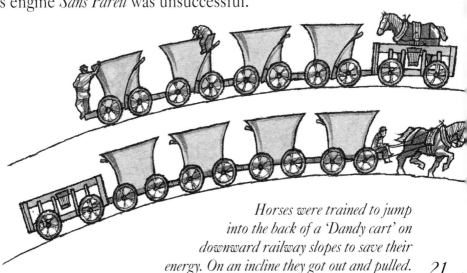

Horses were trained to jump into the back of a 'Dandy cart' on downward railway slopes to save their energy. On an incline they got out and pulled.

THE FIRST INTER-CITY SERVICE

J ohn Farey wrote in 1827: "The high state of wealth and civilisation which the English people have attained within the last half century, has been greatly promoted by the application of the power of the steam engine." In 1830 a steam railway operating a regular passenger service opened. For the first time two major British cities were linked by rail – Liverpool and Manchester. The construction of the line had taken three years. The engineers George Stephenson and his son Robert had found that it was much more complicated than the Stockton to Darlington line.

The engine trials for the new inter-city railway were held in 1829. Robert Stephenson's Rocket *won and continued to work on the Liverpool to Manchester line until 1836.*

A total of 60 bridges had been built and the railway had crossed a wide stretch of peat bog. With the opening of the Liverpool to Manchester line, passenger services on the steam railways had really begun.

Huge crowds gathered to witness the opening of the Liverpool and Manchester Railway on 15 September 1830. Unfortunately there was a fatal accident when Member of Parliament William Huskisson fell into the path of the Rocket.

23

TUNNELS AND BRIDGES

A huge army of navvies bored tunnels and built bridges to create Britain's railway network. In the 18th and 19th centuries the introduction of iron and Portland cement as building materials changed civil engineering design. Before this the only available materials had been stone, brick and timber. Now engineers like the Stephensons and Isambard Kingdom Brunel had much more scope for design as they planned the railways that were to run the length and breadth of Britain and other countries.

Navvies worked in appalling conditions. They dug tunnels by candlelight using only hand tools. Serious accidents were common and there was no system of compensation.

Chaos as passengers and their luggage are shifted from broad gauge carriages to narrow gauge ones.

In 1841 the main line of the Great Western Railway, known as God's Wonderful Railway, was completed from London to Bristol. Brunel designed this line and insisted on a 7ft. gauge, instead of the Stephensons' established 4ft. 8½ in. gauge. This caused major problems for passengers, who had to change trains when joining a new line. Eventually the Stephenson gauge was used all over Britain.

Isambard Kingdom Brunel (1806-1859) was nicknamed the 'Little Giant'.

FIRST, SECOND AND THIRD CLASS PASSENGERS

I t was some time before the comfort of passengers became an important consideration on the railways. Passenger 'carriages' or 'coaches' took their names from the horse-drawn vehicles they replaced. In Victorian Britain, society was rigidly divided into the rich and the poor. This attitude was reflected in the arrangement of seating into separate first, second and third class carriages.

The first Pullman carriage ran in America in 1868. It was a diner; sleepers came later. In June 1874 the Midland Railway introduced Pullman sleepers in Britain. 'Pullman' became a byword for luxury in rail travel.

Early first class travel on the Liverpool to Manchester line.

These paintings show the difference between the way rich and poor people travelled on the railways in late Victorian times.

In the beginning, third class passengers were expected to stand in cold, open-topped trucks but this soon changed.

The first tickets were bronze discs that were collected and reused. Paper tickets were also issued and soon ticket machines started to appear on station platforms.

At first the brakes on carriages had to be operated manually by brakemen sitting on the roof.

Second class passengers sat in open carriages.

SIGNALS AND TIMETABLES

The complex rail network in Britain today is controlled by a computerised signalling system. The first trains were controlled by policemen, who used hand signals or flags to direct trains. Sometimes there were fixed signals that had to be changed by hand. Lamps were used at night – white for 'line clear', green for 'be careful', and red for 'danger'.

In 1838 the London to Birmingham line introduced a post office van. Mail bags were swept into a bag suspended on one side of the train so that the train did not have to stop. Letters were sorted on board. This also speeded up postal communication.

DANGER

CAUTION

*Early
hand signals*

LINE CLEAR

As the rail network grew, signal-boxes were introduced to control train movements. Messages were sent by electric telegraph to the signal-box as a train was approaching. The signalman operated mechanical arms at the side of the track to send a message back to the driver. It was now possible to travel much faster by train than by horse. So that train services could be timetabled, 'standard railway time' was established throughout Britain to replace local time.

YORK Four Days Stage-Coach.

Begins on Friday the 12th of April 1706.

ALL that are desirous to pass from London to York, or from York to London, or any other Place on that Road. Let them Repair to the Black Swan in Holbourn in London, and to the Black Swan in Coney-street in York.

At both which Places, they may be received in a Stage Coach every Monday, Wednesday and Friday, (if God permits.) And sets forth the whole Journey in Four Days, which performs the whole Journey in Four Days, and from Stamford by Huntington to London in two days more. And returns from York to Stamford in two days more. And the like Stages on their return.

Allowing each Passenger 14l. weight, and all above 3d. a Pound.

Performed By { Benjamin Kingman,
Henry Harrison,
Walter Baynes.

Also this gives Notice that Newcastle Stage Coach, sets out from York, every Monday, and Friday, and from Newcastle every Monday, and Friday.

In 1750 London to Edinburgh took 10 days by stagecoach. The train immediately cut this journey to 2 days. By 1850 the journey took 18 hours, by 1855 it was down to 14 hours, and by 1937 it was only 6 hours.

By 1870, 16,000 miles of rail track had been laid in Britain. Track laying continued well into this century. Rail companies had the right to lay track through open countryside. The environment received little consideration.

TRACK LAYING BY NIGHT

29

A DAY AT THE SEASIDE

I n 1841 Thomas Cook set up the first British travel agency and began organising trips to different parts of the world. The Railways Act of 1844 made it compulsory for all railway companies in Britain to run at least one train a day on each of their lines at a fare of a penny (1d) a mile. For ordinary working people, day-trips to the seaside by train became possible when the rail companies offered cheap day-excursion tickets. Seaside resorts expanded, promenades were built and entertainments like Punch and Judy puppet shows became familiar sights. Bank holidays were introduced and large hotels were constructed for wealthy travellers.

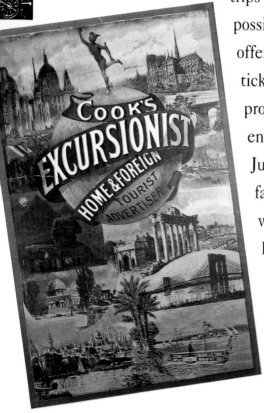

Railways opened up the world to travellers, paving the way for the new travel industry. Thomas Cook conducted his first tour to Egypt in 1869. Cairo became a popular destination.

In Victorian Britain mixed seaside bathing was not allowed.

MIDLAND RAILWAY.

EXCURSIONS to the SEA-SIDE.—SCARBRO', HARROGATE, WHITBY, FILEY, BRIDLINGTON, REDCAR, SALTBURN, WITHERNSEA, The EASTERN COAST, SCOTLAND, MORECAMBE BAY, BELFAST, DUBLIN, ENGLISH LAKES, NORTH WALES, ISLE OF MAN, MATLOCK BATH, BUXTON, MALVERN, &c.

A train full of day-trippers features in this advertisement for the Midland Railway.

From Victorian times onwards, going to the seaside by train was popular in Britain. Posters advertising seaside resorts became more and more colourful and appealing.

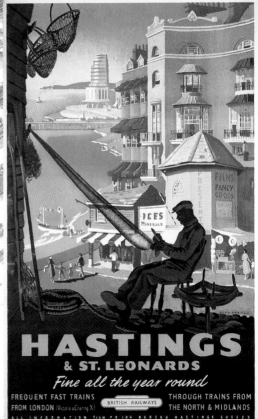

HASTINGS
& ST. LEONARDS
Fine all the year round

| FREQUENT FAST TRAINS FROM LONDON (Victoria & Charing X) | BRITISH RAILWAYS | THROUGH TRAINS FROM THE NORTH & MIDLANDS |

ALL INFORMATION from PR 104 BUREAU HASTINGS SUSSEX

31

BY TRAIN TO THE GREAT EXHIBITION

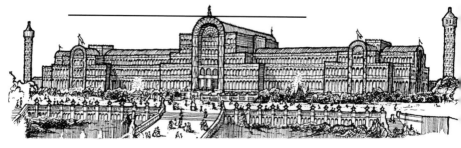

An average of 43,000 people arrived daily at the Great Exhibition to view exhibits from all over the world. Model railways and bridges were on show.

W hen the Great Exhibition opened in 1851 in the Crystal Palace in Hyde Park, London, visitors saw the age of steam, coal and iron on display. In 1854 the Great Exhibition was moved to south London and 5,000 navvies worked on the rebuilding. Its new location was beside the London, Brighton and South railway line. Trains ran right into the grounds.

Thomas Cook encouraged people to travel to the Great Exhibition by train. His firm sold 165,000 excursion tickets and arranged day-trips for over 3,000 school children.

In 1851, steam carriages had carried some visitors through London streets to the Great Exhibition. But these horseless carriages went out of use and horse-drawn carriages and omnibuses once again filled the streets. Single-decker omnibuses had been in use until 1851. But there were so many visitors to the

Exhibition that bus companies had let some passengers travel on the roof – the beginning of the double-decker bus!

After the entry fee to the Great Exhibition was reduced to one shilling (12d), even more people were able to visit it.

33

HOTELS AND STATIONS

The arrival of the railways in Britain effectively did away with canal and stagecoach traffic. Coaching inns were replaced by hotels, as ordinary people discovered the pleasure of travel. Rival railway company advertisements dominated the newspapers. Early in the history of Britain's railways, many of the small pioneer groups had joined together to form a number of important railways running through-routes.

Each railway company had its own coat of arms.

The newsagents WH Smith chartered the first newspaper trains to carry London's newspapers to different parts of Britain. At stations where the train did not stop, bundles of papers were hurled out of the train window on to the platform.

Newly renovated, the Midland Grand Hotel was originally built to serve St. Pancras Station in London. It opened in 1873 and was one of the first hotels to have lifts – known as 'ascending rooms'.

By 1922 there were only four major companies running the whole British rail network. In 1948 British railways were nationalised. The railway that started it all, the Stockton to Darlington line, was part of the NER (the North Eastern Railway) until 1948.

The railways brought long-term employment for many people all over Britain.

TRAMWAYS AND TUBES

The Metropolitan Railway was the first underground rail system. It opened in London in 1863. By 1890 the first electric train had travelled underground from the City of London to south London. But the only real threat to the predominance of rail travel in Britain was the electric street tramcar. The new London Underground rail system worked *with* the railways rather than against them.

The American Civil War was in progress when the Metropolitan Railway opened in 1863. The trains were pulled by steam locomotives, filling the tunnels with sulphur and smoke. Passengers had to carry candles to see in the dark and smoking was forbidden.

Electric locomotives like this one were first used in 1890 on the London Underground rail system – now often called 'the tube'.

Most electric tramcars were double-deckers. This picture shows an old horse-drawn tramcar with a new electric one.

In other countries electrified trains were beginning to take over from steam. By 1914 the age of the steam railway in Britain had reached its peak. The railway companies also owned the steamship services, but things were changing here too and paddle steamers were being replaced by ships with turbines. The maximum speed of express steam trains had reached only 70 mph. Freight trains remained loosely coupled and still lacked continuous brakes.

Diesel-Electric Trains

G eorge Stephenson knew about the power of electricity in 1830 but it was some time before it was used to power trains. Countries like Switzerland, which lacked a regular supply of coal, were the ones that pioneered the electric railway. In 1898 the German engineer Dr Rudolf Diesel patented the diesel engine, making small high-speed engines possible. He shared his ideas with the British, but then mysteriously disappeared in 1913 during the First World War.

This British Intercity 125 *is a diesel-electric locomotive. It has a diesel engine that drives an electric generator. A locomotive is attached to either end of eight coaches and one pushes the train while the other pulls it. This is the fastest type of diesel train in the world.*

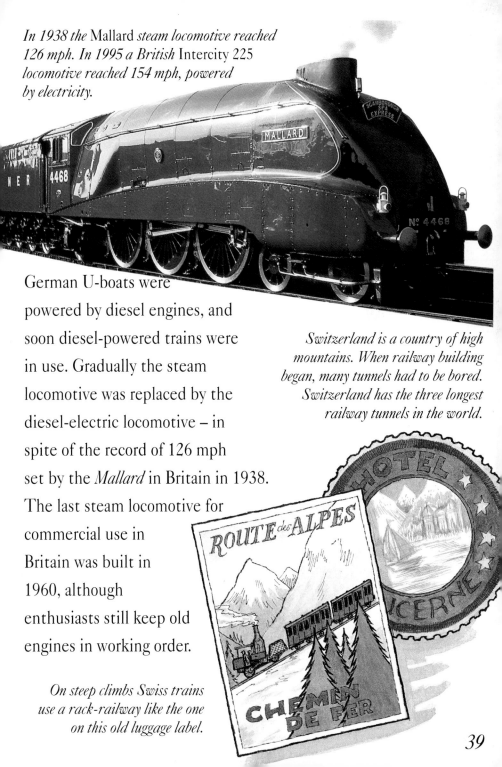

In 1938 the Mallard *steam locomotive reached 126 mph. In 1995 a British* Intercity 225 *locomotive reached 154 mph, powered by electricity.*

German U-boats were powered by diesel engines, and soon diesel-powered trains were in use. Gradually the steam locomotive was replaced by the diesel-electric locomotive – in spite of the record of 126 mph set by the *Mallard* in Britain in 1938. The last steam locomotive for commercial use in Britain was built in 1960, although enthusiasts still keep old engines in working order.

Switzerland is a country of high mountains. When railway building began, many tunnels had to be bored. Switzerland has the three longest railway tunnels in the world.

On steep climbs Swiss trains use a rack-railway like the one on this old luggage label.

FROM AMERICA TO AUSTRALIA

The first railway line across the USA was completed in 1869 when two lines met in Utah – the Union Pacific, built westwards, and the Central Pacific, built eastwards.

From about 1850, railways developed all over the world. On the North American continent the richest source of raw material was wood, so wood-burning locomotives were built. Settlers moving west were soon followed by the railways.

The train on the Normanton-Croydon Railway in Australia is a converted London bus brought to the area in 1930 and still operating. Western Australia also has the longest stretch of straight track in the world – 296 miles across the Nullarbor Plain.

This meant that vast areas of the prairies could be opened up for farming, but the North American Indians were angry at this invasion of their lands. Steam railways were already running in Australia, most of Europe, North Africa, North America and India. Canada's first steam railway opened in 1836, using *The Dorchester* locomotive built by Robert Stephenson. The Canadian-Pacific Railway opened in 1885, linking Montreal with Vancouver – a distance of 2,790 miles.

An American train with a large 'cow-catcher' at the front to push stray cattle out of the way. These trains burnt wood instead of coal.

OPENING UP THE WORLD

The arrival of a railway network in Britain transformed travel, population settlement, and industry. The effects of the Industrial Revolution in Britain were felt across the world. The British iron industry was revived, and later the railways were the biggest market for British steel. Timber was needed for railway sleepers, and a bridge might need as many as a million bricks. British railway engineers built locomotives for many other countries.

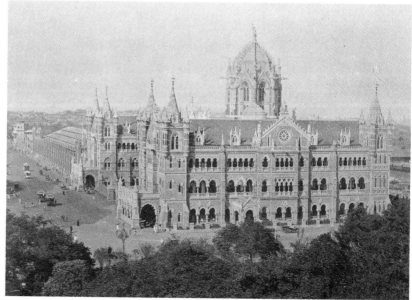

India was part of the British Empire until Independence in 1947. The British introduced a vast steam railway network there and steam trains still run in parts of India today. This wonderful building is Victoria Station in Bombay in the 1890s.

Increase in rail passengers in Britain, 1838-60

1838	5,000,000 PEOPLE
1848	50,000,000 PEOPLE
1860	270,000,000 PEOPLE

Increase in rail freight in Britain, 1855-75

1855	60,000,000 TONS
1865	120,000,000 TONS
1875	180,000,000 TONS

Employment increased as exports grew – these were mostly items of railway equipment for abroad. Without the railways, passenger travel would have remained stagnant until the motor car became available to the general public.

In Britain ordinary people gained a new mobility – not only could they now take holidays but they could also live further away from their place of work. New suburbs grew up around all major towns and cities.

THE ROOF OF LONDON
HAMPSTEAD
TRAVEL BY LONDON'S UNDERGROUND

43

STEAM POWER LIVES ON

S team power is no longer used for mass transportation but it still plays a vital role in today's world – in power stations where it is used to work the generators that produce our electricity. The age of the steam train in Britain came to an end with the introduction of the all-electric train and the diesel-electric train. Although we have high-speed, inter-city train services today, many people now prefer to travel by car and haulage firms carry goods in huge container lorries. Perhaps a new railway age will begin with the arrival of the latest train services through the Channel Tunnel to mainland Europe. But the age of steam has not been forgotten – it is preserved in museums across the world. Some original locomotives still exist and there are working replicas of others.

Britain has many fascinating places to visit to find out more about the railways.

This is one of many studies of stations and steam trains by the famous French impressionist painter Claude Monet.

Enthusiasts all over Britain keep steam trains running. This is one of the engines on the Bluebell Railway in East Sussex, wearing a smiley face for a special children's outing. The carriages look happy too!

GLOSSARY

aqueduct *A bridge-like structure built to carry water over a valley.*

bank holiday *A national day of holiday, first established by Act of Parliament in 1871 in Britain.*

cast iron *Iron containing a lot of carbon, which has to be cast into shape.*

chauldron *A wheeled wagon used to transport coal along railway lines.*

Dandy cart *A three-sided wheeled cart into which a horse jumped to save its energy. Once used on steep rail lines when horse power was essential.*

feet and inches *Imperial measurements no longer widely used in Britain. 1 foot (ft.) = 30.5 cm. 1 inch (in.) = 25.4 mm.*

gauge *The distance between the rails of a railway track.*

Great Exhibition 1851 *An exhibition held in the Crystal Palace in Hyde Park, London, to show manufactured goods from all over the world. It was organised by Prince Albert, husband of Queen Victoria.*

Industrial Revolution *The name given to changes that took place between 1730 and 1850 to transform Britain from an agricultural society into an industrial one.*

Methodism *A Christian organisation begun by John Wesley in 1729.*

omnibus *Now known as a bus. The first omnibuses were horse-drawn.*

Oystermouth Railway *The world's first public passenger railway. It opened on 25 March 1807.*

penny (1d) *The bronze old penny was used in Britain until 1971. 240d = one pound (£1). 12d = one shilling (1s).*

rack-railway *A special railway used on very steep slopes. Cog wheels on the train fit into teeth on the track.*

shilling (12d) *The old British silver shilling was replaced by the current 5p piece in 1971.*

standard railway time *When train timetables were introduced, this replaced local time so that the time was the same all over Britain.*

Watt, James (1736-1819) *A Scottish engineer who created a very successful steam engine that powered machinery in factories and coalmines.*

wrought iron *A pure form of iron containing very little carbon, which is hammered or beaten into shape.*

INDEX